Arena-Taschenbuch

Band 2478

Jürgen Banscherus,
1949 in Remscheid geboren, wollte eigentlich Pianist werden. Leider wurde daraus nichts. Doch inzwischen schreibt er sehr erfolgreiche Kinder- und Jugendbücher und ist gar nicht traurig, dass das mit dem Klavierspielen nicht geklappt hat. Jürgen Banscherus lebt mit seiner Frau und seinen beiden Kindern im Ruhrgebiet.

Ralf Butschkow,
1962 in Berlin geboren, wollte eigentlich Detektiv werden. Er trinkt genauso gerne Milch wie Kwiatkowski, aber leider mag er keine Kaugummis. Deshalb hat er sich für ein Grafikstudium entschieden. Dann arbeitete er ein paar Jahre in Werbeagenturen und ist heute als Kinderbuchillustrator für verschiedene Verlage tätig. Er ist verheiratet und lebt mit seiner Frau und seinen zwei Kindern in Berlin.

Ellen Butzko,
geboren 1963, ist Englischlehrerin an einem Gymnasium, als Fachleiterin auch in der Referendarausbildung tätig und sehr engagiert in der lesedidaktischen Forschung für Fremdsprachen.

Jürgen Banscherus

Kwiatkowski and the chewing gum mystery

Englische Textfassung von Ellen Butzko

Mit Illustrationen von Ralf Butschkow

Arena

1. Auflage als Arena-Taschenbuch 2005

Englische Fassung von *Ein Fall für Kwiatkowski. Die Kaugummiverschwörung*

Englische Fassung: Ellen Butzko

Umschlag- und Innenillustration: Ralf Butschkow
Umschlagtypografie: knaus. büro für konzeptionelle und visuelle identitäten, Würzburg
Gesamtherstellung: Westermann Druck Zwickau GmbH
ISSN 0518-4002
ISBN 3-401-02478-7

www.arena-verlag.de

The chewing gum mystery

private detective – Privatdetektiv
fee – Bezahlung, Honorar
case – Fall
solve a case – einen Fall lösen
disappear – verschwinden
steal – stehlen
someone stole – jemand stahl
professional – Profi
a deal – eine Abmachung
it's a deal – abgemacht
hide – sich verstecken
I hid – ich versteckte mich
fishy – verdächtig
trust my nose – das sagt mir meine Spürnase
somebody was following me – jemand folgte mir
hiding place – Versteck

My name is Kwiatkowski.

I am a private detective.

A tired private detective.

I just got up a few minutes ago.

That means it's time for breakfast:

a glass of milk and a piece of chewing gum.

Not just any chewing gum.

Carpenter's chewing gum.

That's the only good chewing gum.

Everything else tastes like rubber soles.

I've always been a private detective.

rubber soles – Gummisohlen

When I was a baby,
I always found
every piece of Lego
and every sweet
that had disappeared.
I don't know why –
I must have a nose
for finding things.
Take last summer, for example.
Then, too, it was breakfast time.
I had my glass of milk and
then I went looking for
the packet of chewing gum –
empty!
So I went down to Olga's.
I always get my chewing gum at
Olga's.
I am one of her best customers.

customer – Kunde

Olga saw me and said:
"Hi, Kwiatkowski!"
And I answered:
"Hi, Olga. Five packets
of chewing gum
and a lemonade, please." –
"Here's your lemonade, but ..."
I was mildly shocked:
"No Carpenter's?"
Olga said:
"No. Someone steals them. Just
them."
Now I was seriously shocked:
"What? Someone steals Carpenter's
chewing gum?"
Olga said:
"For the last two or three days

mildly – ein bisschen
seriously – ernsthaft

NEWSAGENT

someone has been stealing them.
Nothing else – just them.
I get new ones every day,
but then suddenly they're gone."
I said:
"Maybe you're getting old.
You just can't remember
where you put them."
Olga protested:
"Maybe I'm getting old.
But I'm not daft.
And I've looked everywhere."
I drank my lemonade.
"When will you get
more chewing gum?"
Olga said:
"Tomorrow morning.
You can try

daft – blöd

some other chewing gum for now."

And now I protested:

"No way.

It's either Carpenter's or nothing."

Olga laughed:

"You're really cute, Kwiatkowski."

She wanted to touch me.

Ugh!

I hate that. Nobody touches me!

(I mean Olga is a friend, but that's it.)

And anyway ...

I was thinking.

Thinking about tomorrow.

Olga asked:

"What are you thinking about, cutie?"

I just said:

cute – süß
touch – anfassen
cutie – Süßer

"About tomorrow.
I must find out
who's stealing the chewing gum.
They're professionals.
They steal your chewing gum
from under your nose –
and you don't see
or hear anything."
Olga said:
"Then I must go to the police."
Oh no! Not that!
I said:
"Olga, the police are not interested
in chewing gum.
Let me do it."
And Olga answered:
"You are a darling!"
Oh no! Not again!
She wanted to touch me again!

I quickly said:

"About my fee ..."

Olga began to protest.

I said:

"Only if I find them.

Five packets of Carpenter's.

Is that a deal?"

Olga was happy.

"It's a deal, Kwiatkowski."

The next morning
the alarm rang at 5 o'clock.
No time for breakfast.
There were no Carpenter's today.
Life is dull and grey
without Carpenter's chewing gum.
I went to the fridge
and took a bottle of milk with me.
Mum was still in bed.
Life can be tough
for a private detective.
I went down to Olga's kiosk.

the alarm rang – der Wecker klingelte
dull – öde
fridge – Kühlschrank
tough (sprich: taff) – hart

It was still closed.
There were only
the morning papers
lying in front of it.
I hid behind a bush.
Nobody could see me,
but I could see the kiosk.
The milk bottle stood next to me.
Waiting makes you thirsty.
I waited for an hour.
Then Olga came.
She couldn't see me.
That was good.
Everything was like a normal day.
Nothing looked fishy.
I waited for two
more hours.

thirsty – durstig

A truck came around 8 o'clock.
It brought sweets, crisps, and –
yes, Carpenter's chewing gum.
Olga put all the packets of Carpenter's
on the counter.
Oh, I wanted to have
a piece of chewing gum, just one!
But I had a case to solve.
I drank my milk.
Then I saw three children.
They went up to the kiosk.
They tried to look totally normal.
Fishy, very fishy!
Trust my nose.
The two boys talked to Olga.
Then Olga's head disappeared.
And at that moment

crisps – Kartoffelchips
counter – Theke

the girl climbed onto the counter.
She stuffed all the Carpenter's
into her big bag.
Boy, she was quick.
Then she ran away.
And the boys also ran away.
And Olga? Where was Olga?
She was still looking for something.
I knew it – they were professionals.
And they had stolen MY chewing gum!
I ran after the girl.
She was now walking down the
street – trying to look totally normal.
She stopped at a red light.
I went up to her and said:
"Can I have a piece of chewing gum?"
Wow, she was seriously shocked.
She just wanted to run.

she stuffed – sie stopfte

She almost ran into the cars.
I grabbed her
and pulled her back.
"Are you crazy?" I askcd her.
But she didn't even say 'thank you'!
She shouted at me!
"Leave me alone," she said.
Yeah, in your dreams!
I pulled at her bag.
50 packets of Carpenter's
chewing gum
fell out.
50 packets!
That's enough for two months!
"Why did you steal them?"
No answer.
The girl started to put
the packets back in her bag.

I grabbed her – ich packte sie

"Why did you steal them?"
She was as cool as cucumber:
"Steal them?
I didn't steal them."
I said:
"I saw you. You and your friends.
The two boys talked to Olga
and then you climbed onto the
counter and stole the packets."
She was still quite cool:
"So, let's go to the police."
I answered:
"Don't be daft.
You stole my chewing gum!
Carpenter's is my favourite
chewing gum.
You must give them back to Olga."

as cool as cucumber (sprich: kjukamber) – total cool
(wörtlich: so cool wie eine Gurke)

The girl just stood there.
She was thinking.
Then she said:
"No, I can't do that."
She didn't look at me.
She looked down on the ground.
So I said:
"I'll take them back to Olga."
She looked happier now.
I went on:
"I want to know
why you steal Carpenter's.
Olga has other chewing gum, too."
Again no answer.
I waited.
Then she said:
"Carpenter's is my favourite
chewing gum."

ground – Boden

I looked at her and said:

"Fine. We'll both go to Olga."

She was not very happy about that.

"Okay, okay. Fine.

I steal the chewing gum for

somebody else.

He only wants Carpenter's."

I asked:

"What's his name?"

She answered:

"I don't know his name.

They call him the snake."

So Dick Snake (called "the snake")

was the one I was looking for.

Interesting! Very interesting!

I thought:

I must go home.

I have to think.

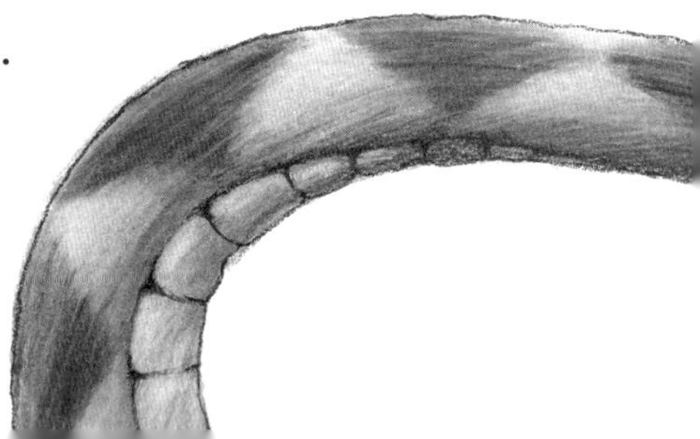

This is a difficult case –
the snake has got
something to do with it.
I said to the girl:
"Give me your bag.
I'll give the chewing gum
back to Olga."
She asked:
"What's your name?
How can I find you?
I want my bag back again."
And I answered:
"My name is
Kwiatkowski.
I live close to Olga's kiosk.
15 Acorn Drive.
And what's your name?"
"My name is Colette," she said.

3

I went back to Olga’s
with 50 packets of Carpenter’s.
”You’re a genius, Kwiatkowski,”
Olga said,
”a total genius.”
I said:
”I don’t have much time.
I have a case to solve.
Give me two packets
of Carpenter’s, please.”
I put the money on
the counter.
Olga protested:
”Your fee was five
packets.

That was our deal."
I just answered:
"Yes, but I haven't solved
the case yet."

I can only think in bed.
In MY bed.
So I put two pieces of chewing gum
into my mouth
and I lay down.

After a while,
I began to see things
more clearly.
Why would the snake
get children
to steal Carpenter's?
And nothing but Carpenter's?
What was Dick Snake's plan?
And what was Colette's role?
The snake was very clever.
Last year I met him
for the first time.
He sold moth balls,
perfectly normal moth balls.
But he told people
they were magic balls.

role – Rolle
moth balls – Mottenkugeln
magic balls – Zauberbälle

It wasn't easy to catch
Dick Snake.
But I am a really good
detective.
He just said:
"Not bad, Kwiatkowski.
Just wait, until we meet
again."
And now I had met him again.
But he didn't know that.
And Colette wouldn't tell him.
Colette!
I didn't know where she lived.
I forgot to ask her.
So – what next?
I had to find out
where the snake was.

meet – treffen, (wieder-)sehen

I remembered that he and his gang
were always hiding
near the slaughterhouse.
But when I went there
I couldn't see him anywhere.
I asked some of the workers.
They hadn't seen him anywhere.
I walked over to the tram stop.
Too much walking
isn't good for a detective.
I thought somebody was following me.
I turned around –
nothing. Everything looked normal.
I still thought something was fishy.
I was glad
when the tram came.

slaughterhouse (sprich: sloterhaus, 'o' wie in Schloss) – Schlachthof
workers – Arbeiter
I turned around – ich drehte mich um

TRAM STOP
SLAUGHTERHOUSE

A man sat next to me
on the tram.
He took a packet of chewing gum
out of his pocket.
Carpenter's chewing gum.
I liked that man.
"That's really good chewing gum,
isn't it?" I asked him.
"It is."
"It's my absolute favourite," I said.
He answered:
"That's interesting.
I tried it two days ago
for the first time."
That *was* interesting!
"Did you get it at Olga's?"
I asked him.
"At Olga's? No.

pocket – (Hosen-)Tasche

I got it from a boy."
I got very excited:
"From a boy!
Where was that?
What did he look
like?"
The man just said:
"At the children's
flea market.
Sorry, I must get
off now."
And then he was gone.
The children's flea
market.
So the snake stole
the chewing gum
to make money
at the flea market.

flea market – Flohmarkt

Or maybe the snake
and Olga had a fight
and that's why he stole
things from her.
I went back to Olga's.
Olga said:
"I've only got one chair.
You can sit on the crate of beer.
Or you can sit on my lap."
Naturally, I sat on the crate of beer.
Then I told her about Dick Snake and
about the flea market.
But Olga didn't know
the snake.
She only knew
that I was a
genius.

crate of beer – Bierkasten

So – what next?

I planned to hide

behind the bush again.

I hoped

the thieves would come again.

This time I would follow them

to the snake.

4

I waited for Colette
for the rest of the day.
I chewed one packet of Carpenter's.
She didn't come.
The next morning
the alarm rang again
at 5 o'clock.
It was raining!
I was *not* happy.
I waited behind my bush
for four hours.
Just a few people came,
but there were no children
and definitely no thieves.
Then I gave up.
I was wet through
and I was very cold.

just a few – nur wenige
wet through – durchnässt

I needed a hot bath now.
I needed to lie in the bath
and think about nothing.
A hot bath always makes me happy.
I was still in the bathroom

when the doorbell rang.
It was Colette!
I was glad
that she had come.
But I was as cool as a cucumber:
"Oh hi."
She was really friendly.
"Hi there."
Then we didn't know
what to say.
"Erm, where is my
bag?"
Colette asked.
I looked behind my bed
and gave her back her
bag.
"Thank you," she said

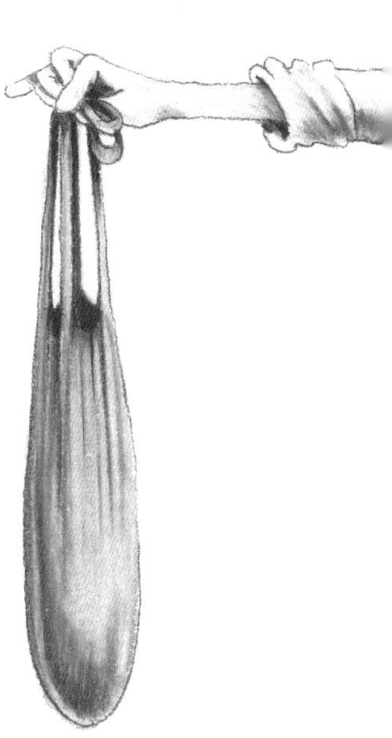

the doorbell rang – es klingelte an der Tür

and went to the door.
I ran after her:
"Wait a second!
I must find the snake.
Do you know where he is?"
She only answered: "No, sorry."
I tried again:
"You owe me something.
I didn't tell Olga
anything about you."
She said:
"Fine. I can only tell you
where we have to deliver
the Carpenter's.
Please don't ever tell the snake
that I told you.
We deliver the chewing gum

owe – schulden
deliver – abliefern

to a bench at the cemetery."
She drew an exact plan.
"We put the packets
in the rubbish bin.
Then we go home.
That's all."
Colette went to the door.
I said:
"Wait. I have got a question.
Why do you steal things for him?
And where do you live?"
Colette said:
"That's two questions.
And it's none of your business,
Quiet Cowboy."

bench – Bank
cemetery (sprich: semitri) – Friedhof
drew – zeichnete
rubbish bin – Abfalleimer
it's none of your business – es geht dich nichts an

"My name is Kwiatkowski,"

I shouted.

But she was gone.

What a nerve!

I thought: I must run after her.

But I had a case to solve.

I had to go to the cemetery.

The cemetery is a long way from my house.

It was around 12 o'clock

when I got there.

There were only a few people there.

what a nerve – was für eine Unverschämtheit

Some brought fresh flowers
to the graves,
others took dead flowers
to the rubbish bins.
Where were the rubbish bin
and the bench
that Colette had talked about?
I looked at her plan:

graves – Gräber

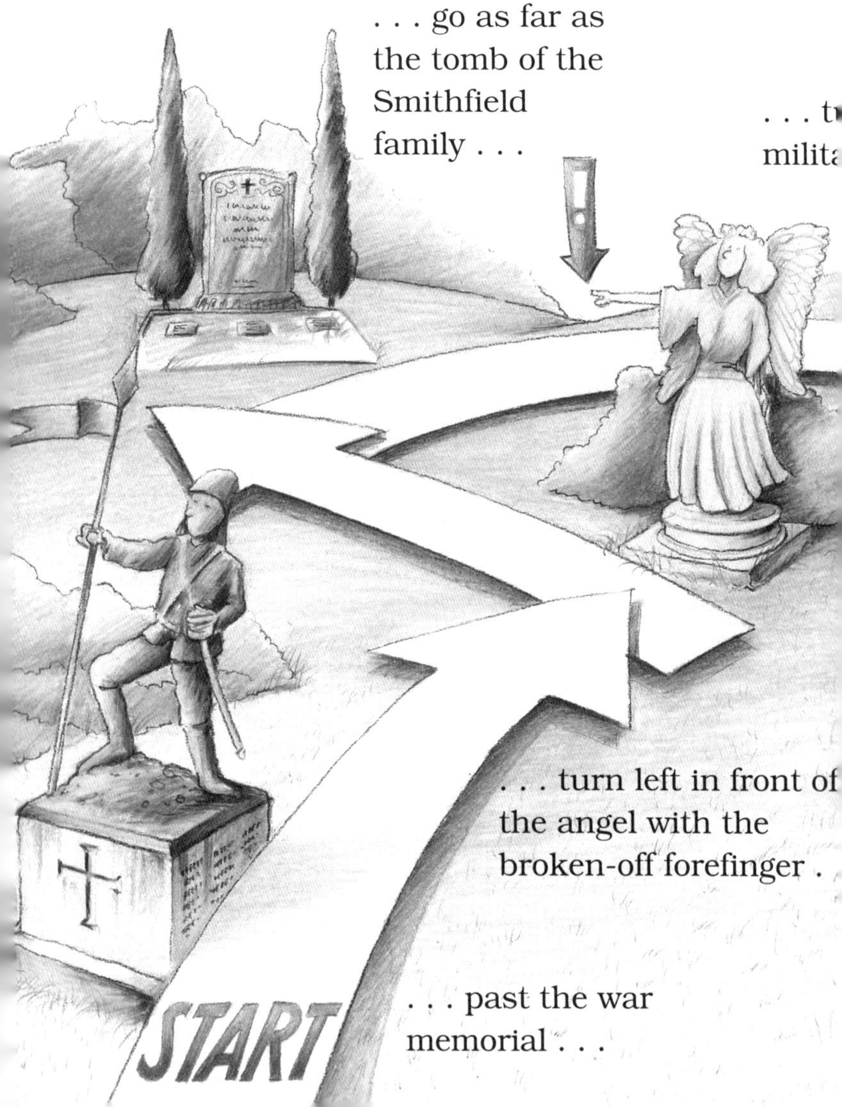

. . . go as far as the tomb of the Smithfield family . . .
. . . t
milit
. . . turn left in front of the angel with the broken-off forefinger .
START
. . . past the war memorial . . .

ight towards the
emetery . . .

. . . you get
to an old
part of the
cemetery . . .

. . . there you'll see a blue
and a green bench . . .

. . . it's the green bench.

The first time
I didn't find the angel.
The second time I got lost
in the military cemetery.
The third time
I found the green bench.
Finally!
What next?
I didn't really know.
I thought: Trust your nose.
I emptied the rubbish bin.
I found:
used tram tickets,
an old newspaper,
dead flowers,
an empty packet of cigarettes.

I got lost – ich verirrte mich
finally – endlich
used – gebrauchte

Useless.

But I trusted my nose.

I looked at the newspaper.

There was the picture of a tank

on the first page.

And next to it

there were two words:

The first word started with an O.

The second word was FACTORY.

Who wrote these two words?

Was it the snake?

Was it

somebody

else?

useless – unbrauchbar

tank – Panzer

factory – Fabrik

I took the newspaper with me.
On my way home I thought:
What is O... FACTORY?
OVEN FACTORY?
ORANGE FACTORY?
ONION FACTORY?
No. Didn't sound right.
OWL FACTORY?
Stupid.
OUTHOUSE FACTORY?
Daft.
I was tired when I got home.
There was a letter from Mum.
She was at work,
so she'd written a letter.

oven – Ofen
onion – Zwiebel
owl (sprich: aul) – Eule
outhouse – Plumpsklo

Hi, great detective!

How's life?

Are you working hard?

Is it a difficult case?

I hope you'll solve it.

Are you hungry?

There are pancakes in the fridge.

You can use the old pan.

Love you, Mum

Pancakes!

Mum really knows

what I like best.

I got the old pan

and put it on the stove.

pancake – Pfannkuchen
pan – Pfanne
stove – Herd

Then I melted some butter
in the pan.
I put the first pancake in the pan.
Something in my head
went 'click'.
I looked at the old pan.
The OLD pan.
Yes. That was it!
OLD FACTORY.
That must be it!
I took the newspaper
out of my pocket.
I looked at the letters.
I even knew where the old factory was.
It is near my school.
Nobody works there now.
The windows are broken

melted – erhitzte

and the roof leaks.
Mum thinks it's dangerous.
It was the perfect hiding place
for the snake.
The old factory –
my nose told me
I would solve my case there.
I ate the two pancakes.
I needed to be strong
to solve my case.

the roof leaks – das Dach ist undicht

5

The old factory isn't
far from my house.
It looks a bit eerie.
When I got there
I couldn't see anybody.
Only an old Coke can.
I went up to one of the doors.
It was locked.
But the windows
were all broken.
So I climbed through
one of the windows.

eerie – (sprich: ihri) unheimlich

The room was very big
and completely empty.
No Carpenter's anywhere.
No sign of the snake anywhere.
There was only dust everywhere.
I walked through the big room.
What was that on the ground?
A piece of paper –
and it looked new!
I picked it up from the floor –
it was a Carpenter's wrapper.
I knew it!
The snake was here somewhere.
I knew I could trust my nose!
I walked towards another door.
There I found another wrapper.

dust – Staub
picked it up – hob es auf
wrapper – (Kaugummi-)Papier, Verpackung

I opened the big door.
It made a horrible creak.
I was inside another big room.
There was a little bit more light in here.
But nothing else.
Again no sign of the Carpenter's.
There was only broken glass on the ground.
From that room I went into a very small, dark room.

it made a horrible creak – sie knarrte schrecklich

And that's where I found it:
a box full of Carpenter's.
I knew it, I thought.
Kwiatkowski, you *are*
a total genius.
You're the greatest detective
since Sherlock Holmes.
Bang. The door behind
me was shut.
"Hello," came a voice from behind me.
I knew that voice.

I turned around.
Dick Snake was
standing at the door
with four boys from
his gang.
I looked around.

voice – Stimme

There were no windows.
There was only the one door.
I was trapped.
"Kwiatkowski, I knew you'd come."
The snake walked up to me.
He was smiling.
"Help yourself," he said
and pointed to the box of Carpenter's.
"It is your favourite chewing gum,
isn't it?
There's lots, so please help yourself."
I didn't know what to say.
He said:
"So, my plan worked perfectly."
I didn't get it:
"Your ... your ... plan?"
He smiled again:

I was trapped – ich saß in der Falle
pointed – zeigte

"You twit.
You're so daft.
You don't get your Carpenter's –
and you stop thinking.
Why don't you use your brain –
just for a minute?
What happened at the kiosk,
the rubbish bin at the cemetery,
the newspaper,
the wrappers on the floor –
all that was my plan.
Brilliant, wasn't it?"
I still didn't get it:
"But if ... the girl stole the Carpenter's
so ... that I would follow her ...
why did you sell the chewing gum
at the flea market?"

twit – Dummkopf
use your brain – denk mal nach

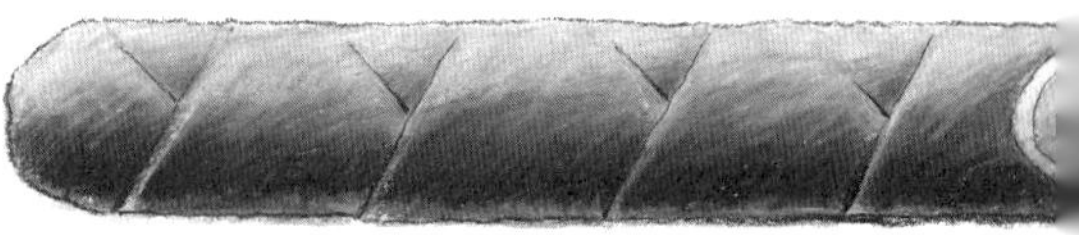

Dick Snake said:
"Bravo, Kwiatkowski. You must be
the greatest detective
since Sherlock Holmes.
That was a little money on the side."
Oh no, he knew everything.
I felt totally stupid.
Was he that clever?
"And why did you do all that?"
He was smiling again.
"Oh, it was fun. So much fun.
And then there is another thing.
Remember last year?
I said we'd meet again.
And I don't forget things.
I warned you."
Then he took a cigar out of his pocket.
It was very thick.
And very long.

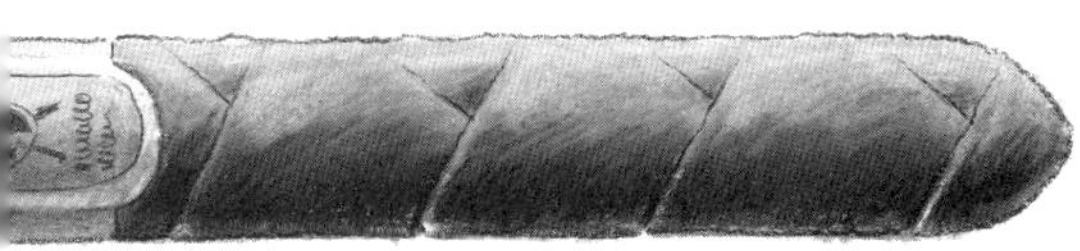

It looked terrible.
"You'll smoke that cigar.
And then you'll never meddle with me again."
I asked:
"What if I say no?"
He pointed to his friends:
"They'll beat you up."
Smoke a cigar?
Get beaten up by four boys?
I didn't like either of them.
I was thinking hard.
Then I said:
"I've got an idea."
The snake laughed:
"You? You've got an idea?"
And I answered:

you'll never meddle with me – du mischst dich nicht mehr ein

"Yes, I have.
Let's have a fair fight."
The snake laughed very loudly:
"You're trapped!
And you want a fair fight?
That's a great idea.
What are you thinking of?"
That was the problem.
My brain was useless.
I only had useless ideas.
I looked down on the ground
and saw the box of Carpenter's.
And there it was, my idea:
"I bet you that
I can blow a bigger bubble
with my chewing gum
than you can."

I bet you – ich wette

The snake said:
"Forget it. You're a professional."
"You can have two pieces of chewing gum,
and I'll only have one," I said.
"I said, forget it," the snake said again.
"You can have three," I said.
The snake laughed:
"Fine, three. But we'll take *my* chewing gum."
What could I say?
Then the snake said:
"If I win, you'll smoke that cigar."
And I said:
"If I win, you'll drink a bottle of soya sauce."
And that was our deal.
One of the snake's friends went

to the supermarket
to buy a bottle of soya sauce.
The snake took a packet
of Hammett's chewing gum
out of his pocket.
He gave me one.
Then he took three for himself.
Hammett's – the world's
most disgusting chewing gum!!!
After a while the boy came back
with a bottle of soya sauce
So we could start.
The snake said:
"Ready, steady, go!"
So we started chewing.
One chewing gum against three.
I didn't think I could win.

most disgusting – der ekligste

I chewed and chewed
to make the gum really thin.
Then I started blowing –
but I had to be very careful.
My bubble was very small.
The snake's bubble was a lot bigger.
His friends were laughing at me.
Then I blew stronger.
My bubble became bigger.
The snake couldn't blow any more.
And my bubble became
bigger still.
It was as big as a
basketball!
Then it burst.

thin – dünn
careful – vorsichtig
it burst – sie platzte

The snake's bubble burst at the same time.

I won!

(With a Hammett's!!!)

The snake said:

"Not bad, Kwiatkowski.

You can go to the circus with that trick."

I only pointed at

the bottle of soya sauce.

Dick Snake didn't look very happy.

He took one sip

and pulled a face.

He paused.

I said:

"Come on, snake,

the whole bottle."

sip – Schluck

he pulled a face – er verzog das Gesicht

And he drank the whole bottle.
"Get lost, Kwiatkowski," he said.
And I answered:
"I'll take the Carpenter's with me."
The snake didn't say
a word.
"What about the
money
from the flea market?"
I asked him.
"No way," he shouted at
me.
Coolly I said: "I'll have to go to
the police then."
So Dick Snake gave me
10 Euro.
What else could he do?

get lost – zieh Leine!

He wanted to say something.
But he couldn't.
He held one hand over his mouth,
one hand over his bottom.
And then he ran.
That was the bottle of soya sauce.
His gang ran after him.
I went outside with my Carpenter's.
And there, all of a sudden, was Colette.
Colette! Everything had started
with her.
She looked at me, then she looked
at the box of Carpenter's.
"They gave you the box – just like
that?"
I said:
"We had a fair fight –
I won"

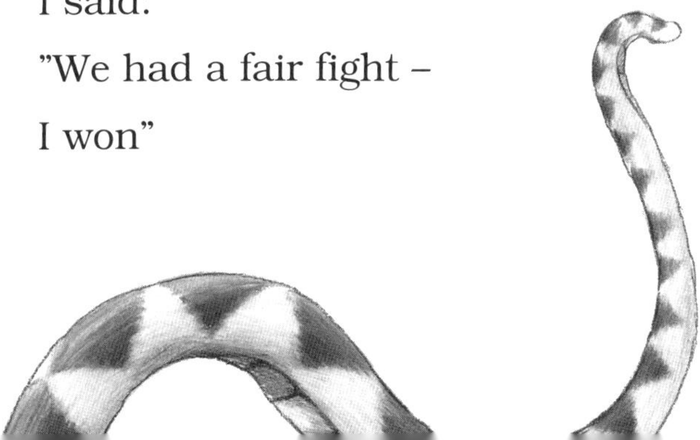

Colette said:
"I don't want to be in the gang anymore. I've had enough of stealing."
I didn't say anything.
And Colette said:
"You don't believe me."
I felt sorry for Colette.
So I said: "Come and have a glass of milk with me at Olga's."
And she said: "Only if I can have lemonade."
We went to Olga's – I had milk and Colette had lemonade.
That was the chewing gum mystery
I didn't see Dick Snake after that.
But I'm not afraid of him.
Private detectives like me need people like the snake.

Hinweise für Eltern und Lehrer:

Dieses Buch basiert auf einem Grundwortschatz von ca. 450 Wörtern. Das entspricht ungefähr zwei Jahren Grundschulenglisch oder einem Dreivierteljahr in einer weiterführenden Schule.
Kinder können in der Fremdsprache viel mehr verstehen, als man bisher immer angenommen hat. Sie achten auf die Wörter, die die Inhalte tragen, nicht auf die grammatischen Wörter. Bei der Übertragung der Kwiatkowski-Abenteuer haben wir besonders viele Wörter benutzt, die ganz ähnlich wie im Deutschen sind (shocked, idea,

detective, packet usw). Auch wenn ein Kind manchmal nur die Hälfte eines Satzes versteht, kann es mithilfe der Bilder, der Ähnlichkeiten zum Deutschen und der Vokabelangaben der Geschichte folgen.

Apropos Vokabelangaben: Sie sollen Hürden abbauen und nicht neue Hürden schaffen. Deshalb sind sie im Unterschied zu den gängigen Englisch-Lehrwerken so verfasst, dass sie teilweise aus ganzen Phrasen bestehen und möglichst wenig grammatisches Wissen von den Lesern abverlangen. Bei ganz ungewöhnlichen Wörtern haben wir die Lautung angegeben, aber bewusst auf die phonetische Transkription verzichtet, weil sie in der Regel für Kinder nicht lesbar ist.

Entscheidend ist also: Sie können Ihrem Kind dieses Buch ruhig schenken, wenn Sie das Gefühl haben, dass es sich für die Abenteuer von Kwiatkowski interessiert. Geben Sie ihm am besten die Lesetipps auf Seite 70 an die Hand.
Die meisten Kinder sind übrigens sehr stolz darauf, wenn sie ihr erstes Buch in einer fremden Sprache gelesen haben – zu Recht.
Also: Viel Spaß und viel Erfolg bei der Lektüre wünschen

Ellen Butzko und Jürgen Banscherus

Lesetipps für Nachwuchs-Detektive

- Wenn du nicht gleich alles verstehst, lies einfach weiter. Du wirst merken, dass du der Geschichte trotzdem folgen kannst.

- Viele neue Wörter, die du vielleicht noch nicht kennst, sind ganz ähnlich wie im Deutschen:
z. B. idea = Idee, brilliant = brillant, start = starten, absolutely = absolut.

- Manche Wörter wirst du wieder erkennen, weil sie im Deutschen auch verwendet werden:
gang, kiosk, clever.

● Vielleicht kennst du ja schon ein deutsches Kwiatkowski-Buch. Dadurch wird vieles leichter, weil du die Fälle schon kennst. Das englische ist ganz ähnlich, aber nicht immer hundertprozentig gleich, also darfst du dich nicht von Kleinigkeiten durcheinander bringen lassen.

● Manche Wörter sind ganz neu, aber darunter werden auch Wörter sein, die einem die Englischlehrerin normalerweise nicht beibringt: z. B. daft = blöd, bescheuert, twit = Dummkopf.